Quilted Garden Delights
Make Your Quilts Bloom—8 Quick Projects

Holly Knott & Diane Knott

C&T PUBLISHING

Text and artwork copyright © 2008 by Holly Knott and Diane Knott

Artwork copyright © 2008 by C&T Publishing, Inc.

PUBLISHER: Amy Marson

EDITORIAL DIRECTOR: Gailen Runge

ACQUISITIONS EDITOR: Jan Grigsby

EDITOR: Liz Aneloski

TECHNICAL EDITORS: Franki Kohler and Nanette Zeller

COPYEDITOR/PROOFREADER: Wordfirm Inc.

COVER DESIGNER/BOOK DESIGNER: Kristen Yenche

PRODUCTION COORDINATORS: Kirstie L. Pettersen and Zinnia Heinzmann

ILLUSTRATOR: Tim Manibusan

Flat quilt and how-to photography by Luke Mulks and Diane Pedersen of C&T Publishing unless otherwise noted

Nature and set-shot photography by Holly Knott

Photo on pages 2–3 courtesy of Photospin

Published by C&T Publishing, Inc., P.O. Box 1456, Lafayette, CA 94549

Library of Congress Cataloging-in-Publication Data

Knott, Holly.

  Quilted garden delights : make your quilts bloom—8 quick projects / Holly Knott, Diane Knott.

    p. cm.

  Includes index.

  ISBN-13: 978-1-57120-448-6 (paper trade : alk. paper)

  ISBN-10: 1-57120-448-2 (paper trade : alk. paper)

  1. Patchwork--Patterns. 2. Quilting--Patterns. 3. Gardens in art. I. Knott, Diane II. Title.

  TT835.K59 2007

  746.46'041--dc22

                                 2007021126

Printed in China

10 9 8 7 6 5 4 3 2 1

Contents

dedication

To my daughter Holly, whose quilted versions of my watercolors have given them a new life. Without her beautiful efforts, this book wouldn't have been possible. To my husband, George, and daughter Danielle, our biggest fans and supporters. To my father, who gave his life in service to our country and didn't live to see the accomplishments of his family. And last but not least, to God, whose gifts are without number.

—Diane

This book is dedicated to several people who are very special to me. First, to my parents, Diane and George Knott, for their constant encouragement of my artistic abilities all my life and for passing on their own artistic and creative genes—Mom's artsy-craftsy genes and Dad's home-remodeling and gardening "jeans" [smile]. And, of course, if my mom weren't such a prolific, talented artist, this book wouldn't have been possible. Second, to my husband, Paul Bokinz. Without his love and support, I wouldn't be in a position to devote all my time to my art. I thank you with all my heart!

—Holly

acknowledgments

We'd both like to thank the people at C&T Publishing for believing in our idea and our artwork for this book. Special thanks go to our editors, Liz Aneloski and Franki Kohler, for their careful reviews and their help in making everything consistent and accurate and to Kristen Yenche for making the book look beautiful.

introduction

Once Diane Knott's watercolor paintings were licensed on quilting fabric, the wheels began turning in her head as she thought of other ways to make her artwork available to quilters. At around the same time, I discovered art quilting and began my exploration of the wonderful world of modern fabrics and what can be done with the beautiful batiks, hand dyes, and other "painterly" fabrics. I started creating artsy quilts with landscape, nature, and architectural themes when I realized that these fabrics provided me with a perfect painterly palette. My mother and I felt that we could join forces and easily re-create some of her simpler garden-themed watercolors as easy-to-make raw-edge appliqué quilts. Many of the fabrics available today will allow you to create quilts that look like watercolor paintings.

Writing this book emphasized how difficult it is for me to follow patterns exactly—even my own! As an art quilter, I like to wing it and often free-form cut my own shapes. I carefully drew the original drawings for this book, only to discover, after laying out the pieces of fabric, that my actual quilt had strayed from my drawing a bit. I had to go back to the drawing board, literally, so I could give you, the reader, an accurate sketch that matched the quilt.

That said, we want you to think of these instructions as mere guidelines that are not set in stone. Although you can follow them exactly if you'd like, you certainly don't have to. We want you to have fun while making these projects. Feel free to change the colors, add additional flowers or leaves or rearrange their placement, alter the borders, and so on. Our instructions will provide you with all the information you need to re-create each project from start to finish, so even a beginner can make the projects, but more-advanced quilters (or adventurous beginners!) can really embellish and revise to their heart's content.

Using the raw-edge fusible appliqué technique explained in this book will allow you to complete these projects quickly. Enjoy your creative time painting with fabric.

general instructions

Our instructions will guide you from start to finish to re-create each of the projects in this book, but we also want you to think of the instructions merely as guidelines and to have fun while making the projects. Feel free to alter the colors, add additional flowers or leaves or rearrange their placement, modify the border widths, and so on. Our instructions will provide you with all the information you need to create each project from start to finish, so even a beginner can make them, but more-advanced quilters (or adventurous beginners!) can really embellish and revise to their heart's content.

SUPPLIES

Fabric

Fabric is such a personal choice. Just thinking about a trip to the quilt shop conjures up images of a wide range of beautiful fabrics—hand dyes, batiks, geometric prints, florals, stripes, plaids, designer collections, silks, home décor fabrics, flannels, quilter's cottons, reproduction fabrics, blenders, metallics—the selection is overwhelming! But it's also wonderful to have that many choices at your fingertips. When you create the projects in this book, you may even want to change the fabrics to suit your own tastes. A vase of flowers could go from painterly to funky if you select polka dot fabric for the vase and plaids for the flowers! Or simply change the colors to match your own décor.

Painterly Fabrics

I generally avoid using solid colors in my quilts. Why? When you observe nature, and even manmade objects around you, you rarely see a true, solid color. Light hitting an object creates light and dark areas, and objects have texture, which also creates light and dark spots. Using various batiks, mottled and tone-on-tone fabrics, hand dyes, and hand dye look-alike fabrics gives you the ability to use fabric as you would paint, without having to know how to paint! Using these types of fabrics will give your quilts life and depth. Just as a painter may not use solid colors when painting, but

would instead apply several hues and shades on one object, you can replicate this effect in your quilts by using these types of fabrics.

 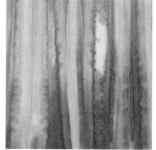

Notice how the hosta leaf shown in this photograph is not solid green. Some parts of it are blue-green, others are yellow-green, and the highlights are almost white.

When you look at the peach daylilies closely, you'll see that they are not really solid peach; nor are their leaves solid green. The petals have shades of peach, pink, beige, and yellow, and even some green closer to their centers. The leaves and stems are dark blue-green as well as yellow-green.

Look for fabrics that convey the texture and color of leaves, for example, without actually having images of leaves on them. Even part of a design, when cut out, can be used for something entirely different. When you get used to thinking this way, you'll begin to "see things" in fabrics. A white fabric with wavy yellow lines might make an excellent flower petal. A batik with pale spots could be used to represent a leaf with a highlight, or a water droplet.

When choosing fabrics for the projects in this book, also think about value (lightness and darkness). Using light, medium, and dark greens for the leaves will make your image look lifelike. Place the darker leaves in the back and the lighter ones in the front.

Choose a background fabric that's lighter or darker than the subject matter of the main image. Batiks, hand dyes, and hand dye look-alikes work well when you want your background to look like a watercolor wash.

They can even make your wallhanging look like a photograph with limited depth of field (subject in focus, background blurred).

Fussy Cutting and Scrap Measurements

Many of the projects in this book call for small scraps of fabric, which is a great way to use up the smaller pieces in your stash. We give you the smallest possible measurement needed for the scrap, but the size can vary slightly depending on how you lay out the pattern pieces and whether you want to do any fussy cutting. For example, five leaf patterns placed side-by-side may require only a 4″ × 10″ piece of fabric, but if arranged differently, they may require an 8″ × 8″ piece or larger. If the fabric has a hand-dyed look with various colors and shades on it, you may need more, so you can fussy cut the five leaves from various locations on the fabric. For pattern pieces that you have to cut several of (or that you might choose to use more of than the instructions call for), such as leaves and flowers, please note that although we provide you with a measurement for the scrap, the size may vary depending on how you choose to cut the fabric and how many leaves and flowers you opt to include.

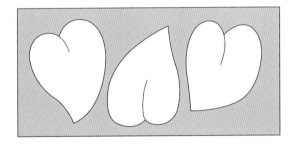

Straight layout

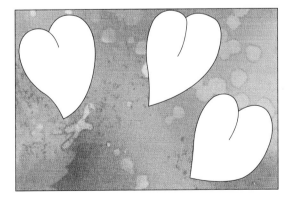

Fussy cut

To Prewash or Not?

I don't prewash my fabrics if I know the quilt will hang on a wall and hopefully will never have to be washed. If there's a good chance that an item will be washed, like a table runner or bed quilt, you should definitely prewash your fabrics. Prewashing can be helpful because fusible web occasionally doesn't stick well to fabrics that haven't been prewashed. I like the crispness of fabrics that haven't been washed, and if I do run into a piece that isn't sticking well to the fusible web, I'll just use a drop or two of fabric glue such as Liquid Stitch by Prym Consumer USA.

Tools and Notions

For the projects in this book, you'll need the following supplies.

* Sewing machine

* Walking foot (recommended for attaching binding)

* Iron

* Small lightbox or a window for tracing

* Thread for piecing

* Thread for appliquéing and quilting

* Scissors

* Rotary cutter

* Ruler

* Large cutting mat

* Paper-backed fusible web
  (I like Pellon's Wonder-Under.)

* Appliqué pressing sheet or nonstick pressing sheet
  (such as The Appliqué Pressing Sheet by Bear Thread Designs), optional

* Graphite transfer paper
  (for *Shhh…Listen to the Rain*)

* Pencil

* Pins

* Tape

* Fabric

* Batting (I like the thinness and drape of Warm & White and Warm & Natural.)

BASIC TECHNIQUES

These instructions apply to all the projects in this book. Refer to the specific measurements for each project.

All piecing instructions assume ¼″ seam allowances.

Background and Borders

In most quilting projects, you add your borders toward the end. In our projects, we add them to the background as the first step because we like to overlap pieces of the main scene onto the borders. The plants and garden objects look like they're growing right out of the main panel!

tip

I like to cut my border strips slightly longer than needed, so I can trim them and square up the piece when I'm done sewing them on. That way there are no worries about having a piece fall short. The measurements provided for border strips in these projects include an extra inch.

Background

Cut your background fabric according to the measurements provided in the project.

Borders

1. Cut your border fabric(s) according to the measurements provided in the project.

2. Sew the first set of strips to the top and bottom of the background fabric, right sides together. Press open. Trim any excess border edges.

3. Sew the second set of strips to the sides of the background fabric, right sides together. Press open. Trim any excess border edges to square up the piece.

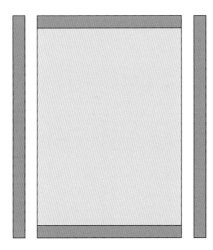

Sew the top and bottom and then sew the sides.

If the piece has a second outer border, follow the instructions given above for the first border.

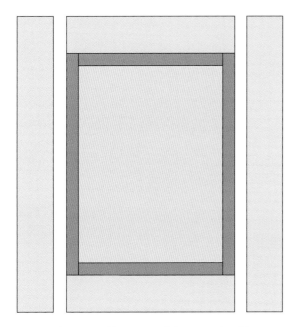

Sew the top and bottom and then sew the sides.

Fusible Appliqué

There are many methods for appliqué—needle-turn, raw-edge (with or without fusible web), freezer paper appliqué, and so on. The projects in this book use the fusible raw-edge method. It's fast and fun! Because seam allowances are not needed with this method, they are *not* included in the appliqué patterns. Should you choose to turn the edges under using a different appliqué method, you'll need to add seam allowances.

All patterns in this book are already printed in reverse so that you can place them under your fusible web, with the paper backing side up, and trace, without having to remember to reverse them.

My favorite fusible web product is Wonder-Under by Pellon. It's a lightweight, paper-backed nylon polyamide. Follow the manufacturer's instructions for applying it to your fabric.

Cutting the Pattern Pieces

1. Using a small lightbox or a window, trace each pattern piece onto the paper side of the fusible web. Be sure to mark each piece with its number or label if it has one! You'll need this information later.

2. Cut out the pattern shapes from the fusible web, leaving at least 1/4″ extra around the edges. That 1/4″ will get cut off, so there's no need to be exact. The point here is just to be able to cover your fabric shapes entirely with the fusible web.

3. Iron the fusible web pieces onto the *back* of your fabric, keeping in mind any particular areas of the fabric you want to use for fussy cutting.

4. Cut out the fabric shapes exactly on the pattern lines. Keep the labeled paper backing attached to the fabric pieces for now.

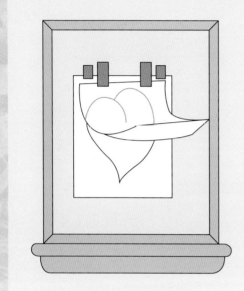
To reduce stiffness when dealing with large pieces (such as the terra-cotta pot in *High Summer*), cut out the pattern shape on your fusible web and then cut out the center portion of the paper leaving just a narrow edge (about $1/2"$ or so) of fusible web, so only the outer edges of the piece will be fused down. Then fuse the piece to your fabric.

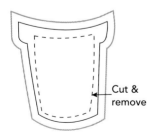

Remove the center of the fusible web.

Fuse to your fabric.

Backing Light-Colored Fabrics

Light-colored fabrics can be somewhat transparent. When you appliqué them over a dark background, the background color might show through and make your light colors look gray or dirty. To prevent this, back the light-colored fabric with inexpensive white cotton.

After ironing the fusible web to your light-colored fabric and cutting out the pattern shape (see Cutting the Pattern Pieces, page 9), cut a piece of white muslin slightly larger than the pattern piece, peel off the fusible web paper from the pattern piece and fuse it to the muslin piece. The light-colored fabric has now been backed with the white fabric. Trim the edges. Then cut another piece of fusible web slightly smaller than the pattern shape and iron it to the white fabric. Peel off the paper. The shape is now ready to be fused down.

Laying Out the Pieces

Once all your pieces are cut out, refer to the placement guide for the project. Two methods are described here for transferring your appliqué pieces to your background or border fabric. Have fun with this part—and *remember that you don't have to be precise.* Rearrange the leaves to your liking, move that garden shovel, or even add a few extra flowers and leaves!

Grid Method

To find the center point of the background fabric, fold it in half left to right, and then in half again top to bottom. Mark the center with a tiny pencil mark if you'd like. The original drawing for each project shows the center point of the quilt. You can use this to help you lay out the pieces.

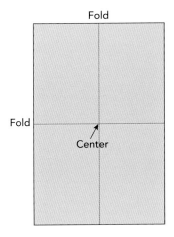

Fold to mark the center.

Pressing Sheet Method

If you prefer, you can photocopy and enlarge the original drawings by the percentage indicated in each project. Place an appliqué pressing sheet (also called a Teflon pressing sheet) over the enlargement. The pressing sheet is see-through! Begin layering the fabric pieces onto it, removing the fusible web's paper backing as you go. Once you're satisfied with the arrangement, iron the pieces in place right on top of the pressing sheet. They'll stick to each other where the fabrics overlap, but they won't stick to the pressing sheet. Then you can move the entire piece as a unit onto your background or border fabric.

The dashed lines shown on some of the individual pattern pieces indicate areas of overlap, but, again, because placement of the pieces isn't critical, use the dashed lines as a guide and don't get hung up on being precise.

Batting and Backing

The instructions for the projects call for batting and backing material to be cut approximately 2″ larger than the finished piece so that if the top piece stretches or shifts a bit as you quilt, you don't end up short on the batting or backing.

Use a thin batting for these wallhangings. I prefer Warm & White or Warm & Natural cotton.

Cut out the batting and backing fabric pieces according to the measurements provided in the project instructions. Place the backing fabric wrong side up on your work table. Place the batting on top of it. Then place your fused quilt top on top of the batting, right side up.

Appliquéing and Quilting in One Step

Ready to Sew!

I like to appliqué and quilt in one step. These projects are small enough that you don't even have to extensively baste the layers together. Pin all the layers together in the area you choose to begin with, or pin the entire piece if you prefer. I use straight pins because they're easier to remove as I'm sewing than safety pins. Begin in or near the center so any excess fabric will get pushed to the edges. When you're done sewing an area, smooth out the fabric and re-pin the next section if any wrinkles have appeared.

Quilting adds another layer of design and texture. It can enhance and define the existing shapes or add a different aspect to them. For example, a quilt made entirely of straight fabric edges and seams can be quilted with curves; the straight lines of the fabric itself almost appear curved!

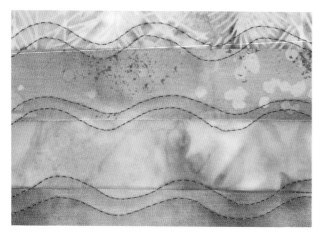

Curves quilted over straight seams

When coming up with ways to quilt my piece, I like to think of the quilting as a layer of drawing on top of the "paint" (fabric), like a pen-and-ink illustration on top of a watercolor wash.

Appliquéing and quilting in one step combines functionality and embellishment. The functionality aspect is that the stitching anchors the fused pieces in place and connects the layers of your quilt. The embellishment aspect is that you can have fun with the thread and "draw" on the fabric. And it's all done in one step, so you can complete your pieces faster.

On leaves and flower petals, you might quilt veins and define outlines with a matching or contrasting thread. On a wooden basket, you might choose a slightly darker thread to outline each slat and add wood grain. Quilt around the edges of a shape to make it pop. Pick up a pattern in the fabric itself, like the swirly shapes in *Elegance* (page 21), and use similar swirly quilting in the background. Each project gives some tips on how you may want to appliqué and quilt your piece in one step.

Choice of Stitches

The stitch options for appliquéing and quilting the pieces are vast! Here are a few of my favorites, with descriptions of when they work best for me.

Straight Stitch

A straight stitch can be used just inside the edges of your fabric shapes.

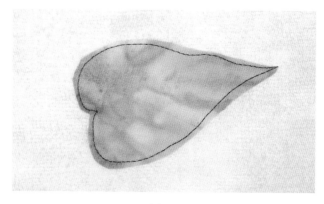

Straight stitch

Blanket Stitch

A blanket stitch gives you the look of hand appliqué without all the work!

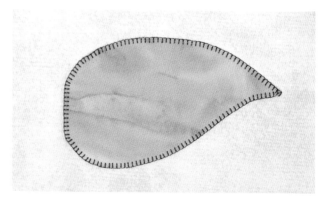

Blanket stitch

Blind Hem Stitch

On my Bernina 153, my preferred blind hem stitch is the #3 stitch with a width of 2 and length of 1. The blind hem stitch enables you to just catch the edge of the appliqué piece with the zigzag portion of the stitch every so often. If you use matching or clear monofilament thread, it's a bit less visible than a regular zigzag stitch and much less visible than a straight stitch.

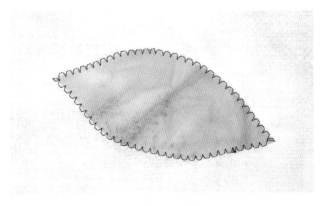

Blind hem stitch

Zigzag Stitch

A zigzag stitch, like the blind hem stitch, can nearly invisibly anchor your pieces in place, especially if you use monofilament thread. Use a tiny stitch length and width for small pieces with a lot of curves. On my Bernina 153, I prefer a stitch width of 2 and a stitch length of 1.25 for zigzag appliqué. An even smaller length (0.25) will create a satin stitch.

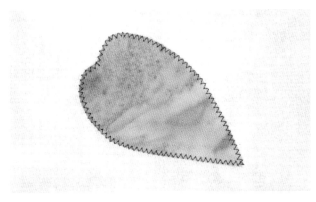

Zigzag stitch

Free-Motion Stitch

Free-motion stitching is done with the feed dogs lowered (or covered on older machines). You control the stitching by moving the fabric in any direction. Creating stippled areas and "drawing with the thread" are done this way. I use free-motion stitching to create veins on leaves, for example.

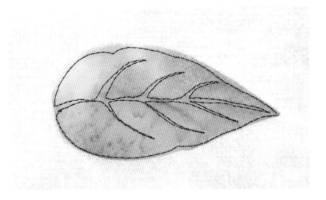

Free-motion stitch

Choice of Thread and Needles
Monofilament

Clear monofilament thread is an excellent choice when you don't want your stitching to be obvious. Perhaps you're trying to anchor some berries and you don't want any visible stitching on them that might interfere with the pattern of the fabric.

When using monofilament, use the smallest needle size possible, or the holes the needle makes in the fabric will be more visible than they would if you were using thicker, colored thread. I like using a 70/10 or a 60/8 needle.

With monofilament, adjust your sewing machine's top tension down a few notches and use cotton thread in the bobbin to help it grab the slick thread. Practice on a small quilt sandwich to get the tension right before you begin work on your actual piece.

If you find that the monofilament breaks during sewing, adjust the tension further and also try placing the spool of thread in a jar or mug and setting it behind the sewing machine.

Colored Rayons

Sulky 40-weight rayon thread with a 70/10 needle is my preference for my appliqué and quilting work, but just like fabric selection, thread selection is a personal preference. You can use any thread that you like. Be sure to use the recommended needle size for that particular brand and weight thread.

tip

Pull the bobbin thread to the top when you begin quilting and clip the ends after you take a couple of stitches. That way the bobbin thread won't get tangled or caught up in your stitching beneath the quilt. Make a few tiny stitches to anchor the thread in place.

tip

Even when fused, some fabrics fray on the edges more than others. On fabrics prone to fuzzy edges, I might use a zigzag or blind hem stitch rather than a straight stitch, which tends to make them fray even more. Or I might even free-motion stitch over the edges, which can also create the illusion of a wavy-edged petal or leaf.

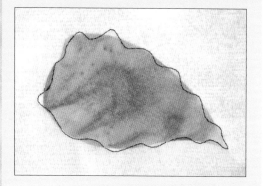

Finishing the Quilt

Binding

The binding measurements provided in the projects are for my back-to-front double-fold method, which makes mitered corners on the front *and* back and doesn't require any hand sewing (a huge plus for me and anyone else wanting to work quickly). However, there are many binding methods, so feel free to use your favorite, in which case you may have to adjust the measurements I give.

tip

You'll be sewing through several layers of fabric and the batting, so use a walking foot to prevent puckering.

1. Trim the edges of your quilt (all layers—the top, batting, and backing) even and square.

2. Refer to the project for measurements. Cut strips of fabric 3″ wide, so that when they are sewn together, the total length of your binding strip will be the measurement indicated on the project pages.

3. Place the strips perpendicular to each other, right sides together, and sew with a diagonal seam. Press open and trim the excess fabric.

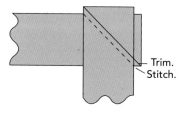

Trim.
Stitch.

Stitch a diagonal seam.

4. Fold the strip lengthwise wrong sides together and press. Open one of the edges and cut it at a 45° angle. Press the edge under. You'll start with this end.

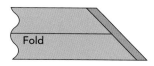

Fold

Cut a 45° angle and press.

5. Place your binding on the *back* of one edge of the quilt, raw edges aligned, and stitch it down using a ¼″ seam allowance, beginning about 4″ from the end of the binding. Stop sewing ¼″ from the first corner. Backstitch. Pull the quilt out of the machine and cut the threads. Fold the binding up (creating a 45° angle) and then fold it back down.

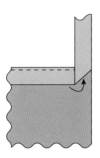

Fold up at 45°.

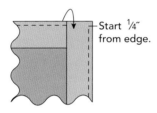

Start ¼″ from edge.

Fold back down.

6. Start sewing ¼″ from the corner where you left off, backstitching a few times. Repeat on all corners. When you reach the beginning of the binding that you left loose, slide the end of the binding into it, trim if necessary, and sew to complete the seam.

7. Now pull the binding toward the front of the quilt, fold it as shown in the illustration, and pin. The mitered corners will form automatically as you fold the fabric around the corners.

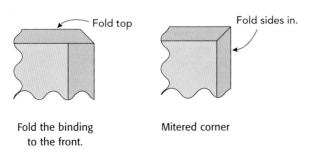

Fold top

Fold sides in.

Fold the binding to the front.

Mitered corner

8. Stitch the binding in place from the front, using a straight stitch right along the edge, a blind hem stitch, or, better yet, a decorative stitch—it'll give you a chance to try out some of those fancy stitches you've never used!

Sample decorative stitches

Labeling

Don't forget to label your creation! First, I sign my quilts right on the front in the lower right corner with a permanent fine point marker. Sharpie and Micron pens work really well. Then I attach a label on the back with more identifying information, such as my name, address, year made, title of piece, and so on. You can buy premade labels and write on them with permanent markers, or create your own. I fuse mine on, but you can also hand stitch them.

Hanging Methods
Hanging Sleeve

1. Cut a piece of fabric the width of your quilt × 4½″. For example, if your quilt is 18″ wide, cut a piece 18″ × 4½″.

2. Turn each of the 4½″ edges under twice and topstitch.

Fold and topstitch.

3. Fold the fabric in half lengthwise, right sides together. Sew the long edge.

Fold in half, right sides together.

4. Turn the sleeve right side out and press. You will have a sleeve that is 2″ high and slightly shorter than the width of the quilt.

5. Pin the sleeve to the back of the quilt just below the top binding. Hand sew in place.

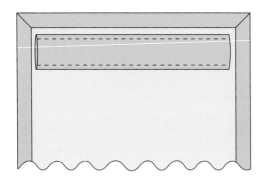

Pin the sleeve to the back of the quilt.

Ways to Display Your Quilt

- Round dowels

Cut the dowel the length of your hanging sleeve. The dowel shouldn't be visible from the front of the quilt. Screw a small eyehook into each end of the dowel. Insert the dowel into the hanging sleeve and place the eyehooks over nails in the wall. Or run picture frame wire between the two eyehooks, so you need only one nail centered behind the piece. Or tie a decorative matching ribbon or a piece of pretty cording onto each eyehook and hang the quilt from one small nail centered above.

Decorative ribbon

- Flat lath strips

Cut the lath a bit longer than the length of your hanging sleeve. The lath should not be visible from the front of the quilt. Drill a small hole in each end of the lath and hang with small nails, or use the ribbon or cording method described above.

- Decorative rod

Cut or buy a decorative rod (like a fluted curtain rod) longer than the width of your quilt so that the rod is visible from the front of the quilt. Finials on the ends look great! Hang the rod from the wall with curtain rod brackets.

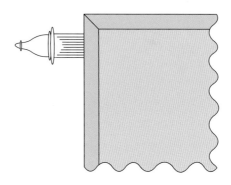

Decorative rod

- Plastic rings

Stitch two plastic rings to the top back corners instead of making a hanging sleeve. Place the rings over nails in the wall.

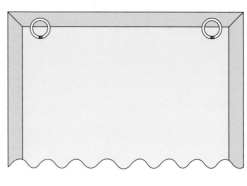

Plastic rings

*I've always loved apple blossoms. One of my favorite
ways to look at them is from under the tree against
a clear and brilliant blue sky. This image was
inspired by springtime and Easter bonnets
and the softness of the season.*

–Diane

apple blossom time

FINISHED SIZE: 18" × 18"

FABRIC

PALE BLUE BACKGROUND:
1 fat quarter

BLUE PLAID BORDER:
1 fat quarter

BASKET HANDLE, VERTICAL SLATS, AND TOP AND BOTTOM STRAPS:
1 fat quarter

GREENERY IN BASKET: 6″ × 9″

HAT: 12″ × 13″

HAT RIBBON: 3″ × 8″

FLOWERS: 8″ × 12″

FLOWER BUDS: 3″ × 6″

LEAVES:
 LIGHT: 3″ × 12″

 MEDIUM: 3″ × 12″

 DARK: 3″ × 12″

BINDING: ⅜ yard

BACKING: 20″ × 20″

BATTING: 20″ × 20″

FUSIBLE WEB (ASSUMING 17″ WIDE): 1¾ yards

6 decorative ½″ buttons for flower centers (optional)

Fabric Selection

When choosing fabric for the leaves, think in terms of light, medium, and dark shades, so you'll have a variety. I used two pink fabrics for the apple blossoms and two darker fabrics for the buds for variety and interest. Notice that the lined pattern I chose for the hat slants to the left on the top of the hat, and to the right on the brim. This deliberate fussy cutting gives the hat more depth. It would have looked too flat if the pattern went in one direction for both pieces.

CUTTING

Pale blue background:
13″ × 13″

Blue plaid border:
2 strips: 3½″ × 14″ (for top and bottom)

2 strips: 3½″ × 20″ (for sides)

Binding:
Cut 3″-wide strips on the straight grain and sew them together, so the length of your strip totals 82″.

CONSTRUCTION
Background and Borders

Use ¼″ seam allowances.

Refer to Background and Borders (page 8) for assembly instructions. Your quilt top should measure 19″ × 19″.

Fusible Appliqué

Refer to Fusible Appliqué (page 9) to prepare the pieces using the 15 patterns on the pattern sheet. Because of the raw-edge technique used, appliqué pattern pieces do not include seam allowances.

There are 2 leaf pattern pieces, but if you flip them over, you'll have 2 additional shapes to choose from. I made 8 leaves from one shape and 9 from the other, but don't feel that you have to follow this exactly. The same goes for the flowers and buds; add more or rearrange them if you'd like.

For the greenery in the basket, draw a rectangle 5½" × 8½" on fusible web, fuse it to the wrong side of the fabric, and cut it out.

Original drawing
For pressing sheet method (page 11) enlarge original drawing 410%.

tips

• The greenery in the basket is a large piece of fabric. To eliminate some stiffness, cut out the 6″ × 9″ rectangle on your fusible appliqué and then cut out the center portion, so that only the outer edges of the greenery will be fused down. (See the illustration in General Instructions page 10.) You could also do the same with the hat top if you'd like.

• Position the basket greenery first and then lay the basket's vertical slats on top of it, followed by the basket's top and bottom straps. I deliberately placed the vertical slats slightly askew to help create the feel of an old basket. Insert the basket handle's edges under the top strap of the basket.

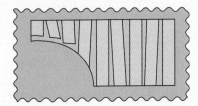

• Lay down the hat's top and bottom sections and then its ribbon. Fuse these in place but don't fuse the basket handle—fuse only the portion that underlaps the basket's top edge. Leave the actual handle loose so you can slide leaves and flowers beneath it. Finally, add the leaves and flowers. Don't feel that you have to be exact—you're creating a flower arrangement of apple blossoms. Have fun with the positioning, and there are no stems to keep track of.

Quilting

Appliquéing and Quilting

Refer to Appliquéing and Quilting in One Step (page 11).

Using white and brown thread, I free-motion quilted highlights and dark areas on the basket slats and handles to give them depth. Green thread was used to satin stitch the stems attached to the buds. The hat was quilted with a darker tan thread to give it dimension. Leaves were given veins, and the pale flowers were outlined with quilting so that they stand out better.

Finishing

Trim the quilt to 18" × 18".

Refer to Binding (page 14).

Refer to Labeling and Hanging Methods (page 15).

Inspiration painting...

I wanted to try something different, simple, and classic but dramatic when I painted this image. It was the first of two matching designs in red and black, and I did another series in pinks and black. Once I got started, I couldn't stop!

—Diane

elegance

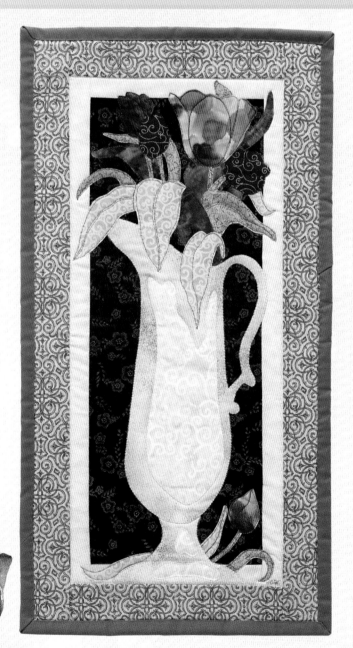

FINISHED SIZE: 14½″ × 26½″

FABRIC

note

The fabric measurements indicated here are the absolute minimum amounts you'll need. In most cases, you can use up scraps from other projects, but larger pieces of fabric might be necessary if you want to fussy cut your shapes.

* *fat quarter = 18″ × 22″*
* *¼ yard = 9″ × 42″*

BLACK BACKGROUND: ⅓ yard

GOLD INNER BORDER: ¼ yard

ARCHITECTURAL OUTER BORDER: ⅜ yard

TULIPS:
  LIGHT (2): 6″ × 6″
  MEDIUM (2): 3″ × 5″
  DARK (1): 3″ × 3″

LEAVES:
  LIGHT (6): 5″ × 12″
  MEDIUM (5): 6″ × 6″
  DARK (5): 6″ × 6″

STEMS: 4″ × 4″

VASE, VASE NECK, AND VASE BASE: 1 fat quarter

VASE HIGHLIGHT: 5″ × 11″

BINDING: ⅜ yard

BACKING: 16½″ × 28½″

BATTING: 16½″ × 28½″

FUSIBLE WEB (ASSUMING 17″ WIDE): ¾ yard

Fabric Selection

When choosing fabric for the leaves, think in terms of light, medium, and dark shades, so you'll have a variety. Place the dark leaves toward the back of the vase, and the light leaves in front. Use the darker leaf fabric for the undersides of the leaves. I used three reds for the tulips for variety and interest, and two of the flowers have some yellow in them to make them stand out more as the focal point flowers and give them more life and interest. The largest tulip also contains the busiest and lightest-colored fabric. The swirly patterns in some of the flowers, leaves, vase, and background add a touch of elegance to the piece, as well as creating a unifying element.

CUTTING

Black background:
8½″ × 21½″

Gold inner border:
2 strips: 1½″ × 9½″ (for top and bottom)

2 strips: 1½″ × 24½″ (for sides)

Architectural outer border:
2 strips: 2¾″ × 11½″ (for top and bottom)

2 strips: 2¾″ × 28½″ (for sides)

Binding:
Cut 3″-wide strips on the straight grain and sew them together so that the length of your strip totals 92″.

CONSTRUCTION

Background and Borders

Use ¼″ seam allowances.

Refer to Background and Borders (page 8) for assembly instructions. Your quilt top should measure 15½″ × 27½″.

Fusible Appliqué

Refer to Fusible Appliqué (page 9) to prepare the pieces using the 32 patterns on the pattern sheet. Because of the raw-edge technique used, appliqué pattern pieces do not include seam allowances.

> *tip*
>
> The vase is a large piece of fabric. To eliminate some stiffness, cut out the pattern shape on your fusible appliqué and then cut out the center portion, so that only the outer edges of the vase will be fused down. (See the illustration in General Instructions page 10.) You could also do the same with the vase highlight.

> *tip*
>
> Place the main body of the vase in position first and then add the vase neck, base, and highlights. Lay out the leaves, stems, and tulips.

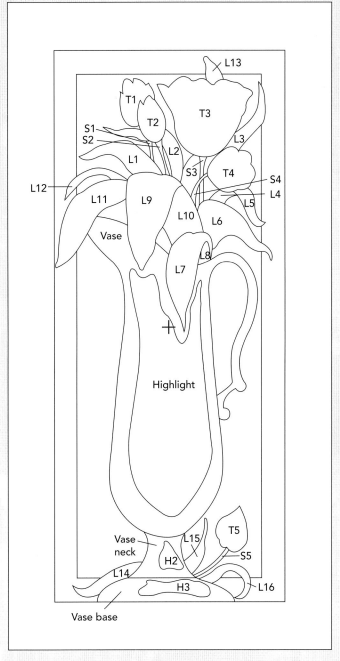

Original drawing
For pressing sheet method (page 11) enlarge original drawing 410%

Quilting

Appliquéing and Quilting

Refer to Appliquéing and Quilting in One Step (page 11).

Using thread darker than the fabric, I free-motion quilted veins on the leaves and defined the petals.

Finishing

Trim the quilt to $14\frac{1}{2}'' \times 26\frac{1}{2}''$.

Refer to Binding (page 14).

Refer to Labeling and Hanging Methods (page 15).

*I was inspired to paint this picture one summer afternoon as I picked
blackberries from the wild bush the birds had seeded in our garden.
My husband and I hated to pull up the bush even though it seemed to want
to encroach on our perennials, so he built a fence for the berries to ramble
over at will. We fertilized and watched as each successive growth increased
in size! Now we'll have lots of berries for jam each summer! I'm delighted
that Legacy Publishing Group has used this painting on greeting cards.*

–Diane

high summer

FINISHED SIZE: 19½" × 25"

FABRIC

note

The fabric measurements indicated here are the absolute minimum amounts you'll need. In most cases, you can use up scraps from other projects, but larger pieces of fabric might be necessary if you want to fussy cut your shapes.

* fat quarter = 18″ × 22″
* ¼ yard = 9″ × 42″

PALE BLUE BACKGROUND: 1 fat quarter

GREEN-BLUE INNER BORDER: 1 fat quarter or ¼ yard

SAGE GREEN OUTER BORDER: ⅜ yard

RAKE: 6½″ × 11″

RAKE HIGHLIGHT: 4″ × 2″

RAKE AND SHOVEL HANDLES: 5″ × 7″

SHOVEL: 5″ × 13″

SHOVEL HIGHLIGHT: 3″ × 8″

RAKE AND SHOVEL KNOBS: 3″ × 4″

FLOWERPOT: 8½″ × 10½″

FLOWERPOT RIM: 10″ × 3″

TEACUP AND HANDLE: 7″ × 11″

TEACUP HIGHLIGHT: 3″ × 5″

BERRIES:
  LIGHTER PURPLE: 8″ × 8″
  DARKER PURPLE: 8″ × 8″

FLOWER PETALS: 12″ × 12″

SMALL GREEN FLOWER BASES: 3″ × 3″

LEAVES L1, L2, AND L3: 12″ × 12″

FLOWER CENTER: 3″ × 3″

SMALL OVAL LEAVES: 4″ × 4″

BINDING: ⅜ yard

BACKING: 21½″ × 27″

BATTING: 21½″ × 27″

FUSIBLE WEB (ASSUMING 17″ WIDE): 1⅔ yards

Fabric Selection

When choosing fabric for the shovel and rake, I used two blue-grays so the shovel and rake would stand out from each other. I also chose a busy print for the berries; the pattern of the fabric makes the tiny berries more visible and simulates the bumps on them. Cutting out the pot and the pot rim from different portions of the same fabric gives the pot a little more interest and makes it look less flat.

CUTTING

Pale blue background:
14½″ × 20″

Green-blue inner border:
2 strips: 1″ × 15½″ (for top and bottom)
2 strips: 1″ × 22″ (for sides)

Sage green outer border:
2 strips: 3″ × 16½″ (for top and bottom)
2 strips: 3″ × 27″ (for sides)

Binding:
Cut 3″-wide strips on the straight grain and sew them together so that the length of your strip totals 99″.

CONSTRUCTION

Background and Borders

Use ¼″ seam allowances.

Refer to Background and Borders (page 8) for assembly instructions. For this project, I fused the flowerpot and its rim onto the background fabric first and then attached the borders so that they cover the right side of the pot. Your quilt top should measure 20½″ × 26″.

Fusible Appliqué

Refer to Fusible Appliqué (page 9) to prepare the pieces using the 22 patterns on pages 53–56. Because of the raw-edge technique used, appliqué pattern pieces do not include seam allowances.

Don't be overwhelmed by the number of berries and flower petals! I included 30 berries in the quilt, but there are only two different shapes. Cut out a variety from the two purple fabrics. And remember that the placement doesn't have to be exact. The same applies to the flower petals. For the larger flowers on the right, there are two petal sizes to choose from. Mix and match with your yellow fabrics and have fun arranging the flowers in the pot.

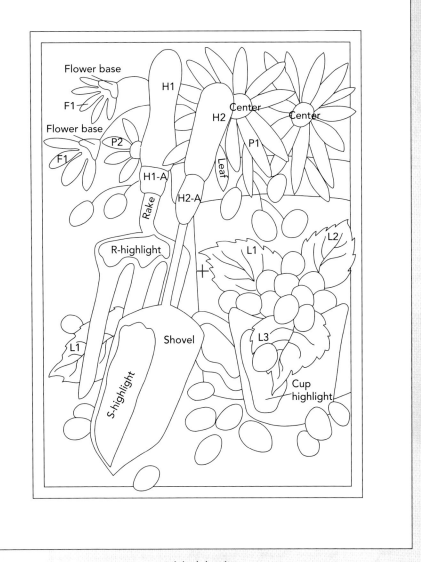

Original drawing
For pressing sheet method (page 11) enlarge original drawing 415%.

tip

The flowerpot is a large piece of fabric. To eliminate some stiffness, cut out the pattern shape on your fusible appliqué and then cut out the center portion, so that only the outer edges of the pot will be fused down. (See the illustration in General Instructions page 10.) You could also do the same with the cup and the shovel blade.

tip

Place the terra-cotta pot and rim in position first. Next add the teacup and handle, leaves, and berries on the front of the pot, rake, shovel, other leaves, flowers, and flower centers and berries.

Appliquéing and Quilting

Refer to Appliquéing and Quilting in One Step (page 11).

I used white zigzag stitching on the shovel to create highlights, and green satin stitching to build the flower stems. Using free-motion quilting, I created shadows, leaf veins, and quilted circular areas on the berries.

Finishing

Trim the quilt to 19½″ × 25″.

Refer to Binding (page 14).

Refer to Labeling and Hanging Methods (page 15).

Quilting

Inspiration painting...

The colors of hydrangeas always seem so soft to me—their softness is very appealing to try to capture in paint. I think it comes across in my watercolor, which pleases me very much. This image has also been used on greeting cards.

—Diane

hydrangea impressions

FINISHED SIZE: 19½" × 19½"

FABRIC

note

The fabric measurements indicated here are the absolute minimum amounts you'll need. In most cases, you can use up scraps from other projects, but larger pieces of fabric might be necessary if you want to fussy cut your shapes.

✳ *fat quarter = 18″ × 22″*

✳ *¼ yard = 9″ × 42″*

PALE BLUE BACKGROUND:
1 fat quarter

DARK GREEN-BLUE INNER BORDER: ⅛ yard or 1 fat quarter

WHITE STRIPED OUTER BORDER:
1 fat quarter or ⅜ yard

BASKET, HANDLES, AND RIM:
1 fat quarter

TAN WORN SPOTS ON BASKET:
3″ × 6″

SHADOW UNDER BASKET:
4″ × 17″

RAKE: 6″ × 3″

SHOVEL: 5″ × 3″

RAKE AND SHOVEL HANDLES:
2½″ × 4″

HYDRANGEAS:
  LIGHT (2): 5″ × 8″
  MEDIUM (3): 5″ × 12″
  DARK (2): 5″ × 8″

LEAVES:
  LIGHT (4): 12″ × 12″
  MEDIUM (7): 12″ × 12″
  DARK (8): 12″ × 12″

STEM: 1″ × 4″

BINDING: ⅜ yard

BACKING: 21½″ × 21½″

BATTING: 21½″ × 21½″

FUSIBLE WEB (ASSUMING 17″ WIDE): 2 yards

2 small decorative buttons for basket "hinge"

Fabric Selection

When choosing fabric for the leaves, think in terms of light, medium, and dark shades, so you'll have a variety. Place the dark leaves toward the back and inner portion of the basket, and the lights in front. The fabric I chose for the leaves is a dusty blue-green to tie the leaves into the basket, border, and background colors.

CUTTING

Pale blue background:
14″ × 14″

Dark green-blue inner border:
2 strips: 1″ × 15″ (for top and bottom)
2 strips: 1″ × 16″ (for sides)

White striped outer border:
2 strips: 3¼″ × 16″ (for top and bottom)
2 strips: 3¼″ × 21½″ (for sides)

Binding:
Cut 3″-wide strips on the straight grain and sew them together so that the length of your strip totals 88″.

CONSTRUCTION

Background and Borders

Use ¼″ seam allowances.

Refer to Background and Borders (page 8) for assembly instructions. Your quilt top should measure 20½″ × 20½″.

Fusible Appliqué

Refer to Fusible Appliqué (page 9) to prepare the pieces using the 17 patterns on the pattern sheet. Because of the raw-edge technique used, appliqué pattern pieces do not include seam allowances.

tip

The basket is a large piece of fabric. To eliminate some stiffness, cut out the pattern shape on your fusible appliqué and then cut out the center portion, so that only the outer edges of the basket will be fused down. (See the illustration in General Instructions page 10.)

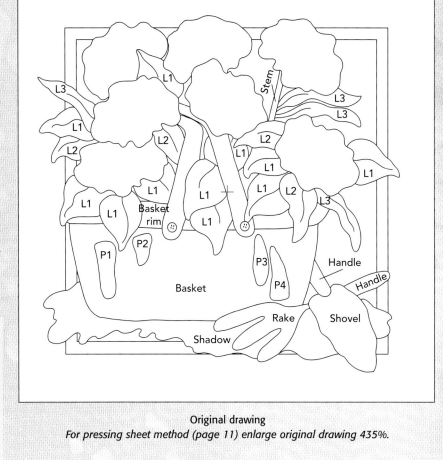

Original drawing
For pressing sheet method (page 11) enlarge original drawing 435%.

tip

Place the basket and its shadow in position first, followed by the garden tools. Fuse. Next lay down the basket's rim, handles, and the flowers, and finally, arrange the leaves around them. Place some of the dark leaves in the center so that the flowers pop out from the background. Don't worry about overlaps or making the arrangement match the quilt sample exactly. Have fun with it—you're creating a fabric floral arrangement!

Appliquéing and Quilting

Refer to Appliquéing and Quilting in One Step (page 11).

I quilted random swirls on the flowers to give them some depth, and I used a free-motion straight stitch on the basket to simulate the grain.

Finishing

Hand sew the buttons on.

Trim the quilt to $19^{1}/_{2}$″ × $19^{1}/_{2}$″.

Refer to Binding (page 14).

Refer to Labeling and Hanging Methods (page 15).

Quilting

Inspiration painting...

This is another image inspired by the textures of a country garden. Gardening is one of my favorite pastimes, as long as the day is cool! This was one of those days when I set my gardening aside in order to paint—instant gratification instead of waiting for the seeds to sprout!

—Diane

planting time!

FINISHED SIZE: 16½" × 21½"

FABRIC

note

The fabric measurements indicated here are the absolute minimum amounts you'll need. In most cases, you can use up scraps from other projects, but larger pieces of fabric might be necessary if you want to fussy cut your shapes.

✳ *fat quarter = 18˝ × 22˝*

✳ *¼ yard = 9˝ × 42˝*

PEACH BACKGROUND:
1 fat quarter

MAROON INNER BORDER AND HORIZONTAL STRAPS FOR BASKET:
1 fat quarter or ¼ yard

PALE GREEN OUTER BORDER AND WOOD HANDLE ON BASKET:
³⁄₈ yard

BIRDHOUSE PEAK AND BASE:
10˝ × 10˝

BIRDHOUSE OPENING: 2˝ × 2˝

BASKET:
GREEN VERTICAL SLATS:
4˝ × 18˝

OFF-WHITE CROCK: 7˝ × 8˝

SHOVEL BLADE: 5˝ × 7˝

SHOVEL HANDLE: 1˝ × 7˝

RAKE: 4˝ × 6˝

GLOVE: 5˝ × 5˝

SEED PACKETS: 5˝ × 10˝

3 FLORAL PRINTS FOR CENTERS OF SEED PACKETS: 3˝ × 4˝ each

HERBS SIGN: 3˝ × 6˝

HERBS SIGN STAKE: 2˝ × 8˝

HERBS SIGN LETTERING: 3˝ × 5˝

STRAWBERRIES: 4˝ × 6˝

STRAWBERRY STEMS: 3˝ × 4½˝

BINDING: ³⁄₈ yard

BACKING: 18½˝ × 23½˝

BATTING: 18½˝ × 23½˝

FUSIBLE WEB (ASSUMING 17˝ WIDE): 1½ yards

DARK CORDING FOR BASKET HANDLE: ⅝ yard

FABRIC GLUE (optional)

Fabric Selection

When choosing fabric for the basket and birdhouse, my goal was to find fabrics that looked weathered. A soft, country-style plaid was used for the glove. I used two different pink fabrics for the strawberries for interest and depth.

CUTTING

Peach background:
11½˝ × 16½˝

Maroon inner border:
2 strips: 1˝ × 12½˝ (for top and bottom)

2 strips: 1˝ × 18½˝ (for sides)

Pale green outer border:
2 strips: 3˝ × 13½˝ (for top and bottom)

2 strips: 3˝ × 23½˝ (for sides)

Binding:
Cut 3˝-wide strips on the straight grain and sew them together so that the length of your strip totals 86˝.

CONSTRUCTION

Background and Borders

Use ¼" seam allowances.

Refer to Background and Borders (page 8) for assembly instructions. Your quilt top should measure 17½" × 22½".

Fusible Appliqué

Refer to Fusible Appliqué (page 9) to prepare the pieces using the 14 patterns on the pattern sheet. Because of the raw-edge technique used, appliqué pattern pieces do not include seam allowances.

Cut 4 of the right angled vertical basket slats and then flip the pattern piece over and cut 3 of the left-facing slats. Cut 2 of the basket center wedges.

Cut 3 rectangles, 3" × 4", for seed packet backgrounds. Using floral fabrics, cut 3 rectangles, 2" × 3", for seed packet center images. Fuse the packet centers onto the larger packet backgrounds. Cut a 4½" × 6½" rectangle for the birdhouse base. Cut a ½" × 6½" strip for the herbs sign stake.

 tip

The birdhouse, crock, and shovel blade are large pieces of fabric. To eliminate some stiffness, cut out the pattern shapes on your fusible appliqué and then cut out the center portions of them, so that only their outer edges will be fused down. (See the illustration in General Instructions page 10.)

tip

Position the birdhouse pieces first, followed by the basket pieces (see the illustration for help with basket arrangement). Fuse them down but don't fuse the top basket strap yet (so you can slide the seed packets underneath it). Position the seed packets in the basket and fuse (including the top basket strap). Place the herbs stake, sign, and lettering. Fuse. Next place the rake, crock, and glove. Fuse. Position the shovel and handle and the strawberries. Fuse. Lay down the cording for the basket handle pieces after you do the appliquéing and quilting.

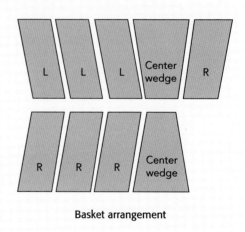

Basket arrangement

Quilting

Appliquéing and Quilting

Refer to Appliquéing and Quilting in One Step (page 11).

Using maroon thread, I free-motion quilted the fingers on the glove to give it depth. Monofilament thread was used to stitch down the word "herbs." Satin stitching around the birdhouse, crock, and seed packets defines their edges.

Arrange the cording for the handle and tack it in place with fabric glue or pins. Hand or machine stitch. Fuse the basket handle in place and quilt.

Finishing

Trim the quilt to $16\frac{1}{2}" \times 21\frac{1}{2}"$.

Refer to Binding (page 14).

Refer to Labeling and Hanging Methods (page 15).

Original drawing
For pressing sheet method (page 11) enlarge original drawing 440%.

Inspiration painting...
*I'm just in love with the color red!
I also love to work with textures. I had
so much fun painting this picture and
incorporating my favorite color with
the textures of the basket and leaves.*

–Diane

serendipity summer

FINISHED SIZE: 22″ × 22″

FABRIC

note

The fabric measurements indicated here are the absolute minimum amounts you'll need. In most cases, you can use up scraps from other projects, but larger pieces of fabric might be necessary if you want to fussy cut your shapes.

✳ *fat quarter = 18″ × 22″*
✳ *¼ yard = 9″ × 42″*

BROWN BACKGROUND:
1 fat quarter

PEACH INNER BORDER:
1 fat quarter or ¼ yard

BROWN OUTER BORDER: ⅜ yard

BASKET: 7″ × 11″

BASKET HANDLES AND RIM:
3″ × 11″

BABY'S BREATH (WHITE FLOWERS): 12″ × 14″

LEAVES:
  LIGHT: 12″ × 12″

MEDIUM: 12″ × 12″

DARK: 12″ × 12″

FLOWERS: 9″ × 9″

PEARS: 7″ × 9″

PEAR SHADOWS (P3 AND P4):
2″ × 3″

BINDING: ⅜ yard

BACKING: 24″ × 24″

BATTING: 24″ × 24″

FUSIBLE WEB (ASSUMING 17″ WIDE): 1¾ yards

Fabric Selection

When choosing fabric for the leaves, think in terms of light, medium, and dark shades, so you'll have a variety. I used a pretty basket-weave print for the basket, but if you can't find something similar, a wood grain or even a mottled tan would work nicely. You can always simulate the weave with quilting.

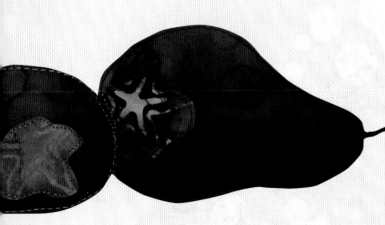

CUTTING

Brown background:
18″ × 18″

Peach inner border:
2 strips: 1″ × 19″ (for top and bottom)
2 strips: 1″ × 20″ (for sides)

Brown outer border:
2 strips: 2½″ × 20″ (for top and bottom)
2 strips: 2½″ × 24″ (for sides)

Binding:
Cut 3″ wide strips on the straight grain and sew them together so that the length of your strip totals 98″.

CONSTRUCTION
Background and Borders

Use ¼″ seam allowances.

Refer to Background and Borders (page 8) for assembly instructions. Your quilt top should measure 23″ × 23″.

Fusible Appliqué

Refer to Fusible Appliqué (page 9) to prepare the pieces using the 19 patterns on the pattern sheet. Because of the raw-edge technique used, appliqué pattern pieces do not include seam allowances.

This project might look a little complicated, but not to worry—think loose, painterly, random, and have fun making this fabric flower arrangement! There are no stems, and you don't have to place any of the flowers or leaves in the same positions that I did.

I used 47 leaves in the quilt, but there are only 4 different leaf shapes. I cut about 12 leaves of each shape, with ⅓ of them being dark, ⅓ medium, and ⅓ light green. You can even free-cut your leaves and not use the pattern at all. There are also 14 flowers, but only 1 pattern shape. Remember, the placement doesn't have to be exact.

tip

The basket is a large piece of fabric. To eliminate some stiffness, cut out the pattern shape on your fusible appliqué and then cut out the center portion, so that only the outer edges of the basket will be fused down. (See the illustration in General Instructions page 10.)

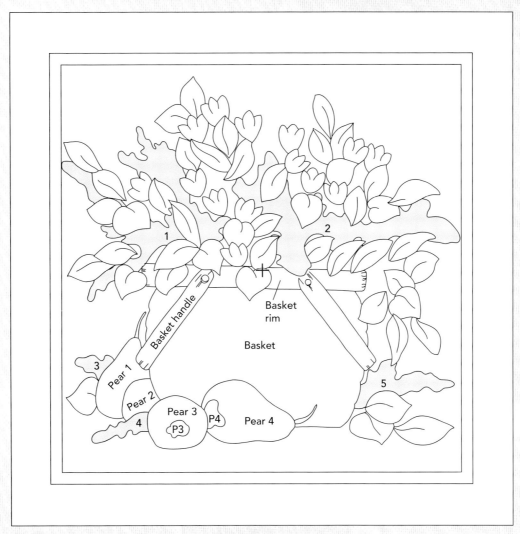

Original drawing
For pressing sheet method (page 11) enlarge original drawing 410%.

tip

Place the basket in position first. Next add its rim and handles, followed by the baby's breath and the pears. Finally, add the leaves and flowers.

tip

Place the darker part of the pear fabric toward the bottom to simulate shading.

Appliquéing and Quilting

Refer to Appliquéing and Quilting in One Step (page 11).

Using coordinating green threads, I machine quilted veins in the leaves and used a simple echo quilting technique in the background. Echo quilting is created by outlining the outer edges of the pieces, matching their shapes with your stitching. I used brown thread and a tight zigzag stitch to apply stems to the pears.

Finishing

Trim the quilt to 22″ × 22″.

Refer to Binding (page 14).

Refer to Labeling and Hanging Methods (page 15).

Quilting

Inspiration painting...

*What could be softer and more gentle
than a fresh spring rain! That's what I tried
to convey in this image of spring icons.*

–Diane

shhh...listen to the rain

FINISHED SIZE: 17″ × 21″

FABRIC

* fat quarter = 18″ × 22″
* ¼ yard = 9″ × 42″

PALE YELLOW BACKGROUND: 1 fat quarter

PALE BLUE INNER AND OUTER BORDERS (SAME FABRIC): ⅝ yard

DARK BLUE MIDDLE BORDER: ⅛ yard

WATERING CAN: 9″ × 11″

WATERING CAN NECK: 4″ × 11″

WATERING CAN SPOUT (PEACH): 2″ × 4″

FUSSY-CUT FLOWER ON WATERING CAN: 4″ diameter maximum

BLUEBIRD:
    BACK/WING (BLUE): 2″ × 4″
    BELLY (PEACH): 2″ × 3″

LEAVES:
    LIGHT: 4″ × 18″
    DARK: 4″ × 18″

BERRIES: 6″ × 6″

BINDING: ⅜ yard

BACKING: 19″ × 23″

BATTING: 19″ × 23″

FUSIBLE WEB (ASSUMING 17″ WIDE): 1⅛ yards

CORDING FOR WATERING CAN HANDLE (FLAT BRAIDED OR SATIN WOULD WORK WELL): ¾ yard

THIN WHITE COTTON TO BACK THE YELLOW BACKGROUND FABRIC: 1 fat quarter or a 10½″ × 14½″ piece

GRAPHITE TRANSFER PAPER (can be found in an art supply store or craft store in the drawing section, and many quilt shops carry this as well)

FABRIC GLUE (optional)

Fabric Selection

When choosing fabric for the leaves, think in terms of light and dark shades, so you'll have a variety. I used two different blues for the watering can to create depth and interest, and I used the same peach fabric for the watering can spout, some of the berries, and the bluebird's belly to tie them together. The same pale blue fabric was used for the background and the outer border.

CUTTING AND CONSTRUCTION

Use ¼″ seam allowances.

This project is put together a little differently from the others in this book. For the others, you attach the borders to the background fabric first, do all the fusing, and then do your stitching. But because Diane's painting has the look of a torn piece of paper in the background, we used the following steps to simulate that look in fabric. The finished piece will be a little stiff because of the multiple layers, but you should be able to stitch through them just fine. You'll also be doing a little stitching before you layer the quilt with the batting and backing material, whereas in the other projects the quilting is handled last.

Cut pale blue border:
13″ × 17″

Cut pale yellow background:
10½″ × 14½″

Cut thin white cotton:
10½″ × 14½″

Because the pale yellow background fabric will be fused on top of the pale blue border fabric, the blue color might show through a bit, making the yellow look dingy or gray. To prevent this, back the yellow fabric with the white cotton:

Cut 2 pieces of fusible web about 10¼″ × 14¼″ (just slightly smaller than the yellow and white fabrics, so it doesn't stick to your iron when you fuse it). Iron 1 piece to the back of the yellow background fabric. Peel off the paper, place the white fabric on top of the fusible adhesive on the yellow fabric, and iron. The yellow fabric is now backed with the white fabric. Next, iron the second piece of fusible web to the white fabric.

Torn Paper Edges

Keeping in mind the torn paper look, cut free-form wavy edges on this fabric sandwich, using the original drawing for reference (no need to be exact).

Peel off the fusible paper, center the yellow-and-white fabric sandwich yellow side up on top of the 13″ × 17″ pale blue border fabric, and fuse in place.

Using a satin stitch and tan thread, stitch around the edges of the yellow fabric. Because of the thickness of the fabric and the fusible web, you shouldn't need a stabilizer.

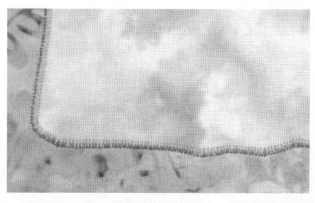

Satin stitch

Fusible Appliqué

Refer to Fusible Appliqué (page 9) to prepare the pieces using the 9 patterns on the pattern sheet. Because of the raw-edge technique used, appliqué pattern pieces do not include seam allowances.

tip

The watering can is a large piece of fabric. To eliminate some stiffness, cut out the pattern shape on your fusible appliqué and then cut out the center portion, so that only the outer edges of the can will be fused down. (See the illustration in General Instructions page 10.)

1. Cut out the watering can, neck, and spout, making sure to cut the circle out of the center of the can. Arrange these 3 pieces in place and iron them, leaving the top inch of the can un-ironed for now.

2. Transfer the outlines of the stems and swirls using the graphite transfer paper. Place the transfer paper on top of your quilt and position the stem and swirl outline drawings where appropriate, referring to the original drawing. You may want to use a lightbox or window so you can see through the layers. Using a pencil with a not-too-sharp tip, trace the stems and swirls. The transfer paper will transfer their image onto your fabric.

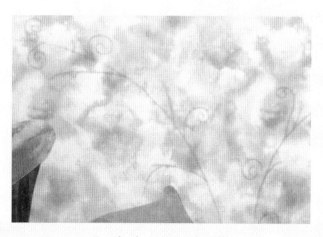

Transfer the stems and swirls.

3. Using free-motion quilting, stitch the stems and swirls. Lift the top portion of the watering can and start your stitching underneath it. Don't worry about backtracking on a line (something you might not typically do when quilting a regular quilt). These stems need to be thicker than one stitch width anyway, and you're drawing with thread.

Stitch the stems and swirls.

4. Satin stitch around the edge of the circle on the watering can. Fussy cut a flower or flowers no larger than 4″ in diameter to go inside the circle and fuse them down.

5. Cut out the leaves. There are 2 leaf shapes, but if you flip them over, you'll have 4 shapes to choose from. Arrange them in place and fuse.

Original drawing
For pressing sheet method (page 11) enlarge original drawing 400%.

note

Although the berries, handle, and bird have not been placed yet, you'll move on to adding the outer 2 borders, followed by appliquéing and quilting. It's easier to quilt the leaves without the handle and berries covering several of them.

Borders

Here you'll add the narrow dark blue border, followed by the outer pale blue border. (I used the same fabric here that I used for the first border the pale yellow fabric was fused to.)

Cut dark blue narrow border fabric:

2 pieces: 1″ × 14″ (for top and bottom)

2 pieces: 1″ × 19″ (for sides)

Cut pale blue border fabric:

2 strips: 2½″ × 15″ (for top and bottom)

2 strips: 2½″ × 23″ (for sides)

Refer to Background and Borders (page 8) for assembly instructions. Your quilt top should measure 18″ × 22″.

Appliquéing and Quilting

Refer to Appliquéing and Quilting in One Step (page 11).

1. Using coordinating green threads, I free-motion quilted veins on the leaves. I used blue thread to stitch around the edge of the watering can, and I used clear monofilament thread to stitch down the fussy-cut flowers.

Quilting

2. Arrange the cording for the handle, referring to the original drawing, and tack it in place with fabric glue or pins. Hand or machine stitch.

3. Finally, position the berries in place (I used 28 berries and clear monofilament thread to stitch them) and arrange the bird pieces on top of the handle and quilt them down. I used a satin stitch for his eyes, legs, and beak. To create the triangular shape of the beak, narrow the stitch as you get closer to the tip.

Finishing

Trim the quilt to 17″ × 21½″

Cut 3″-wide strips of fabric on the straight grain and sew them together so that the length of your strip totals 86″. Refer to Binding (page 14).

Refer to Labeling and Hanging Methods (page 15).

Shhh . . . Listen to the Rain
Stems & Swirls
Stitching Diagrams

Just when the winter blahs have become too much, I am ready to paint the cheerful colors of spring. Yellow tulips made me think of sunshine and warmer days ahead. Maybe there were still bare brown branches outside my studio window, but inside my studio, these bright colors bloomed on my desktop! They've found their way onto house flags to welcome spring outside many houses around the country.

–Diane

spring is sprouting

FINISHED SIZE: 17" × 21½"

FABRIC

note

The fabric measurements indicated here are the absolute minimum amounts you'll need. In most cases, you can use up scraps from other projects, but larger pieces of fabric might be necessary if you want to fussy cut your shapes.

✳ *fat quarter = 18″ × 22″*

✳ *¼ yard = 9″ × 42″*

PALE YELLOW BACKGROUND: 1 fat quarter

YELLOW BORDER: ⅜ yard

TERRA-COTTA POT AND RIM: 11″ × 12″

POT HIGHLIGHTS AND PATINA: 5″ × 11″

LEAVES:
  LIGHT: 12″ × 12″
  MEDIUM: 8″ × 8″
  DARK: 9″ × 6″

TULIPS:
  LIGHT: 6″ × 6″
  MEDIUM: 8″ × 8″

  DARK: 8″ × 8″

CENTERS (4): 6″ × 8″

BINDING: ⅜ yard

BACKING: 19″ × 23½″

BATTING: 19″ × 23½″

FUSIBLE WEB (ASSUMING 17″ WIDE): 1⅜ yards

BLACK CORDING FOR WIRE BASKET (FLAT BRAIDED OR SATIN WOULD WORK WELL): 3½ yards

PURPLE TULLE FOR SHADING ON POT (optional): 6″ × 12″

FABRIC GLUE (optional)

Fabric Selection

When choosing fabric for the leaves, think in terms of light, medium, and dark shades, so you'll have a variety. Place the dark leaves toward the back of the pot, and the lights in front. I used three different yellows for the tulips for variety and interest, and the centers of the flowers have a surprising splash of pink in them. I also used a yellow-green for the leaves to tie them in with the yellow background, border, and flowers.

Cutting out the pot and the pot rim from different portions of the same fabric gives the pot a little more interest and makes it look less flat.

CUTTING

Pale yellow background:
13″ × 17½″

Yellow border:
2 strips: 3″ × 14″ (for top and bottom)
2 strips: 3″ × 23½″ (for sides)

Binding:
Cut 3″-wide strips on the straight grain and sew them together so that the length of your strip totals 87″.

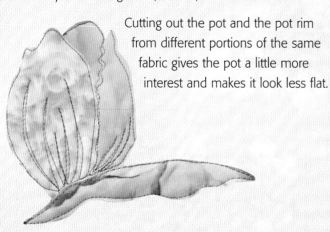

CONSTRUCTION

Background and Borders

Use ¼″ seam allowances.

Refer to Background and Borders (page 8) for assembly instructions. Your quilt top should measure 18″ × 22½″.

Fusible Appliqué

Refer to Fusible Appliqué (page 9) to prepare the pieces using the 33 patterns on the pattern sheet. Because of the raw-edge technique used, appliqué pattern pieces do not include seam allowances.

tip

The terra-cotta pot is a large piece. To eliminate some stiffness, cut out the pattern shape on your fusible appliqué and then cut out the center portion, so that only the outer edges of the pot will be fused down. (See the illustration in General Instructions page 10.)

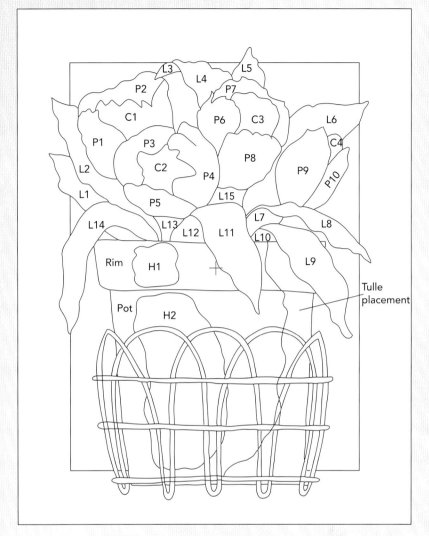

Original drawing
For pressing sheet method (page 11) enlarge original drawing 400%.

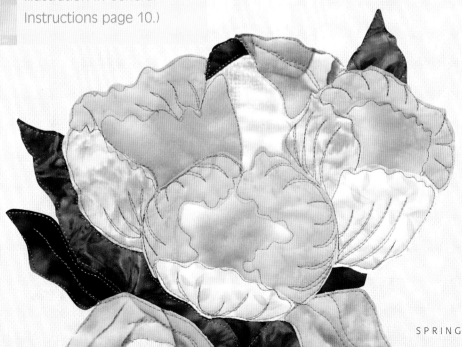

tip

Place the terra-cotta pot and its rim in position first and then add its highlights and patina. Next add the dark and medium leaves, followed by the light leaves, the rear 2 tulips, the front left tulip, and finally the tulip on the right.

If you want to create a shadow on the pot, cut the tulle larger than you need (about 4″ × 11″), pin it in place (refer to original drawing on page 49), and stitch around the edges using a matching purple or clear monofilament thread and a straight stitch. Trim the tulle close to the stitching. Be very careful when ironing the piece now because the tulle will melt! Avoid that area.

Appliquéing and Quilting

Refer to Appliquéing and Quilting in One Step (page 11).

1. Using thread darker than the fabric, I free-motion quilted veins on the leaves and defined the petals.

2. Refer to the quilt photo and the original drawing (page 49) to position the black cording to simulate the wire basket. Using a soft pencil, mark the dots on your fabric. Position the cording and tack it in place with fabric glue or pins. Hand or machine stitch.

Finishing

Trim the quilt to 17″ × 21½″

Refer to Binding (page 14).

Refer to Labeling and Hanging Methods (page 15).

Quilting

Index

For more information, ask for a free catalog:

C&T Publishing

P.O. Box 1456

Lafayette, CA 94549

(800) 284-1114

email: ctinfo@ctpub.com

website: www.ctpub.com

For quilting supplies:

Cotton Patch

1025 Brown Ave.

Lafayette, CA 94549

(800) 835-4418 or

(925) 283-7883

email: CottonPa@aol.com

website: www.quiltusa.com

About the Authors

Holly Knott (Diane's daughter) is a Finger Lakes, New York, artist who could never call just one medium her own. After leaving behind her seventeen-year career as an interactive systems designer and usability testing specialist in New Jersey, she now works full time in a wide variety of media, including art quilting, photography, painting, and website and graphic design. Inspiration for her work comes from her surroundings, including her love of architecture old and new, rural landscapes, and nature in all forms. She feels that being involved in various art forms can only enhance an artist's work because they're all interconnected.

Her painterly art quilts of landscape, nature, and architectural scenes are exhibited in juried quilt and art shows nationwide, have won awards, and are sold in local shops and arts centers. Her artwork has appeared in several publications, including *Quilting Arts Magazine* and in a 2007 calendar of works by women artists. She has also been a contributing writer to *Quilting Arts Magazine.*

Holly lives with her husband, Paul Bokinz, and their two cats on a small "farmette" in the scenic Finger Lakes region of New York. You can see more of Holly's artwork on her website: www.hollyknott.com.

Diane Knott can't remember a time when she didn't want to be an artist. Her earlier years, spent in the home of her grandparents, inspired most of her kitchen and garden images. Today, she and husband, George, live in the beautiful Pennsylvania mountains in a small cottage overlooking lush hills and valleys, farms, and woods. These views, her home and garden, and her growing years are constant sources of inspirational material for her ever-growing portfolio. Today, as a full-time watercolorist, she has her images produced on a variety of licensed products that continue to grow in number. Diane licenses her art exclusively through the energetic and highly successful team of Linda McDonald, Inc. Diane also has several successful fabric collections with Clothworks Textiles, and more are in the works.

Diane and George have two daughters, Holly and Danielle. Holly is the co-author of this book, and Danielle, a talented singer, is currently an editor for a theological publishing company. You can see more of Diane's artwork on her website: www.dianeknott.com.

Great Titles
from C&T PUBLISHING

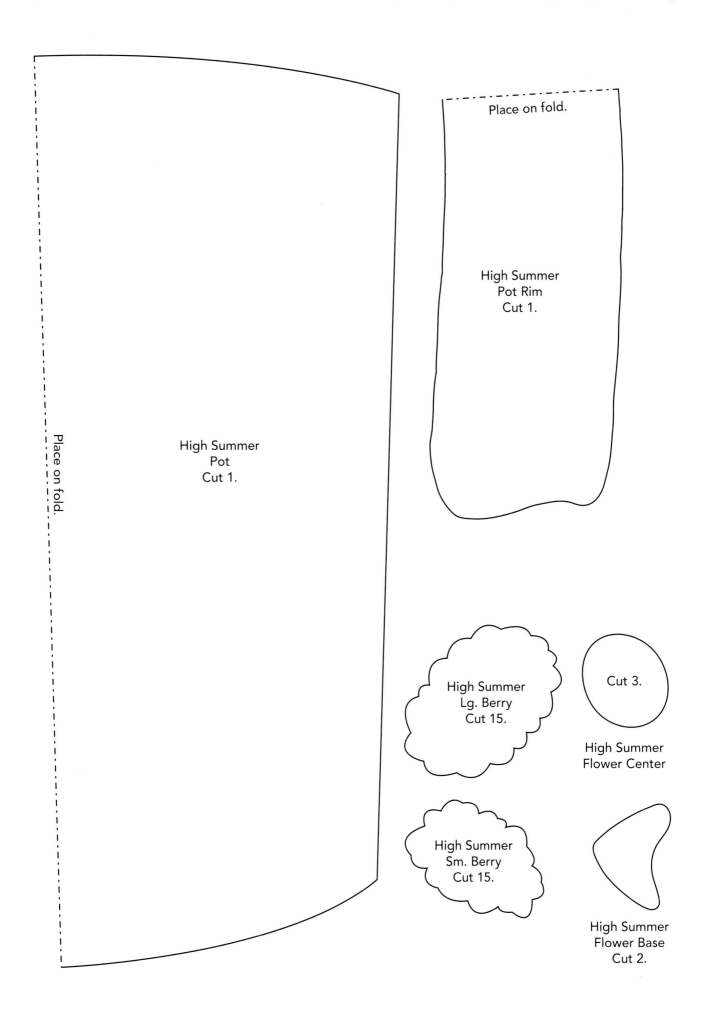

Place on fold.

High Summer
Pot
Cut 1.

Place on fold.

Place on fold.

High Summer
Pot Rim
Cut 1.

High Summer
Lg. Berry
Cut 15.

Cut 3.

High Summer
Flower Center

High Summer
Sm. Berry
Cut 15.

High Summer
Flower Base
Cut 2.

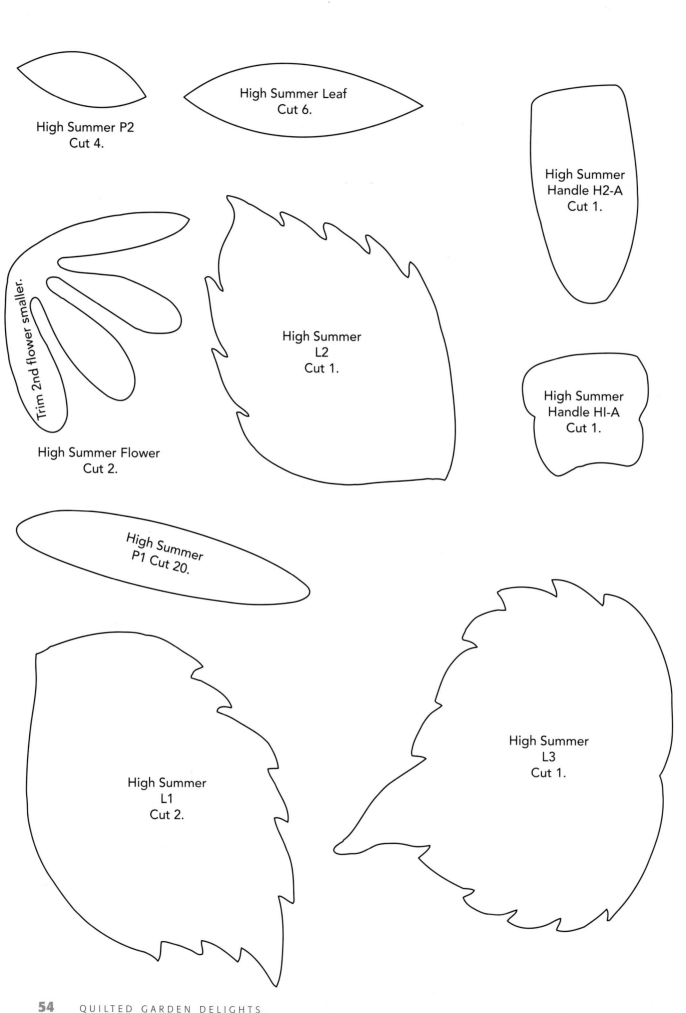

High Summer P2
Cut 4.

High Summer Leaf
Cut 6.

High Summer
Handle H2-A
Cut 1.

Trim 2nd flower smaller.

High Summer
L2
Cut 1.

High Summer
Handle HI-A
Cut 1.

High Summer Flower
Cut 2.

High Summer
P1 Cut 20.

High Summer
L1
Cut 2.

High Summer
L3
Cut 1.

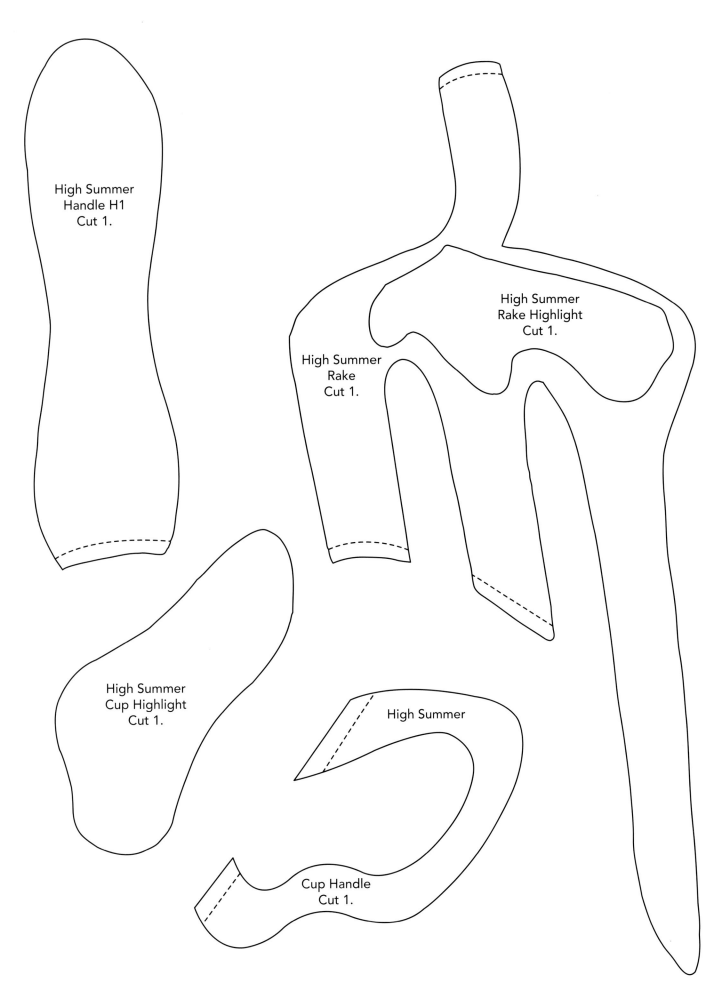

High Summer
Handle H1
Cut 1.

High Summer
Rake Highlight
Cut 1.

High Summer
Rake
Cut 1.

High Summer
Cup Highlight
Cut 1.

High Summer

Cup Handle
Cut 1.

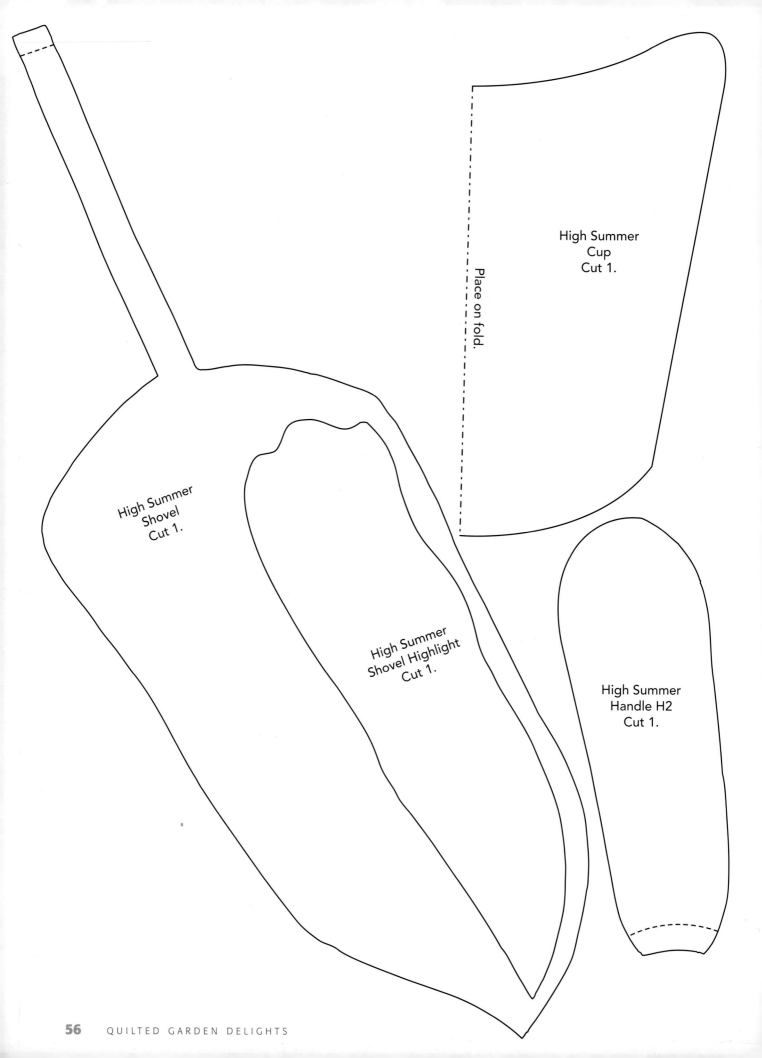

High Summer
Cup
Cut 1.

Place on fold.

High Summer
Shovel
Cut 1.

High Summer
Shovel Highlight
Cut 1.

High Summer
Handle H2
Cut 1.